Level 1

Pictures for Language and Literacy Support

McGraw Hill SRA

Bothell, WA • Chicago, IL • Columbus, OH • New York, NY

Photo Credits

01 Jules Frazier/Getty Images; 02 C. Borland/PhotoLink/Getty Images; 03 Steve Mason/Getty Images; 04 Brand X Pictures; 05 CORBIS; 06 Pixtal/age footstock; 07 Photodisc/Getty Images; 08 Pixtal/age footstock; 09 PhotoLink/Photodisc/Getty Images; 10 Photodisc/Getty Images; 11 Pixtal/age footstock; 12 Digital Vision/Getty Images; 13 DLILLC/CORBIS; 14 Geostock/Getty Images; 15 Creatas/PictureQuest; 16 CORBIS; 17 Photodisc/Getty Images; 18 Creatas/PunchStock; 19 Nick Koudis/Getty Images; 20 Comstock Images/Getty Images; 21 imagebroker/Alamy; 22 bobo/Alamy; 23 S. Solum/PhotoLink/Getty Images; 24 Jacques Cornell/The McGraw-Hill Companies; 25 Getty Images; 26 Radlund & Associates/Getty Images; 27 CORBIS; 28 Pixtal/age footstock; 29 Lawrence M. Sawyer/Getty Images; 30 C Squared Studios/Getty Images; 31 Digital Archive Japan/Alamy; 32 Stockdisc; 33 Ingram Publishing/SuperStock; 34 Siede Preis/Getty Images; 35 Ingram Publishing/SuperStock; 36 Andy Crawford/Getty Images; 37 Digital Zoo/Digital Vision/Getty Images; 38 Purestock/Getty Images; 39 Photodisc/Getty Images; 40 Andrew Leyerle/Getty Images; 41 Stockdisc/PunchStock; 42 Thurid Ems/Getty Images; 43 Stockbyte/Getty Images; 44 Ryan McVay/Getty Images; 45 Stockbyte/Getty Images; 46 Steve Sant/Alamy; 47 Ingram Publishing/SuperStock; 48 Chemistry/Getty Images; 49 Stockbyte; 50 Photodisc Inc./Getty Images; 51 Dimitri Vervitsiotis/Getty Images; 52 IT Stock/PunchStock; 53 Lee Karney/U. S. Fish and Wildlife Service; 54 William Leaman/Alamy; 55 Brand X Pictures/PunchStock; 56 Arthur S. Aubry/Getty Images; 57 ImageState/Alamy; 58 Comstock Images/Getty Images; 59 Creatas/PunchStock; 60 PhotoConcepts/the Agency Collection/Getty Images; 61 Getty Images; 62 Dave King/Dorling Kindersley/Getty Images; 63 Brian Hagiwara/Brand X Pictures/Getty Images; 64 D. Hurst/Alamy; 65 Jules Frazier/Getty Images; 66 Jan Csernoch/Alamy; 67 Getty Images; 68 Ariel Skelley/Blend Images/CORBIS; 69 Ingram Publishing/Fotosearch; 70 Creatas/PunchStock; 71 G.K. & Vikki Hart/Getty Images; 72 Joshua Ets-Hokin/Getty Images; 73 Stockbyte/Getty Images; 74 Ryan McVay/Getty Images; 75 Image 100/CORBIS; 76 Image Source/Punchstock; 77 D. Hurst/Alamy; 78 Nino Mascardi/Photographer's Choice/Getty Images; 79 ZenShui/Sigrid Olsson/PhotoAlto Agency RF Collections/Getty Images; 80 Blend Images/Getty Images; 81 Ingram Publishing; 82 Jupiterimages/Comstock Images/Getty Images; 83 Stephen Ogilvy/The McGraw-Hill Companies; 84, 85 Photographer's Choice RF/Getty Images; 86 Paul Burns/Photodisc/Getty Images; 87 Jupiterimages/Comstock Images/Getty Images; 88 C Squared Studios/Getty Images; 89 Paul Miles/Axiom Photographic Agency/ Getty Images; 90 Charles Smith/Yellow/CORBIS; 91 Ingram Publishing/SuperStock; 92 Raimund Koch/Stockbyte/Getty Images; 93 Ingram Publishing; 94 Stockbyte/PictureQuest; 95 Koki Iino/Getty Images; 96 Steve Hamblin/Alamy; 97 Mitch Hrdlicka/Getty Images; 98 photosindia/Getty Images; 99 Colin Paterson/Digital Vision/Getty Images; 100 Kari Marttila/Alamy; 101 David Frazier/ Yellow/CORBIS; 102 Sue Scott/Oxford Scientific/Getty Images; 103 Patrick Byrd/Alamy; 104 Lilli Day/Photodisc/Getty Images; 105 Barbara Penoyar/Photodisc/Getty Images; 106 Alexandra Grablewski/Photodisc/Getty Images; 107 Steve Hamblin/Alamy; 108 Photodisc/Getty Images; 109 Karl Weatherly/Photodisc/Getty Images; 110 R. Strange/PhotoLink/Stockbyte/Getty Images; 111 Jeff Rotman/Iconica/Getty Images; 112 Tinke Hamming/Ingram Publishing; 113 Goodshoot/Jupiterimages; 114 Burke/Triolo Productions/Brand X Pictures/Getty Images; 115 Frank & Joyce Burek/Photodisc/Getty Images; 116 Alastair MacEwen/Oxford Scientific/Getty Images; 117 Digital Archive Japan/Alamy; 118 SuperStock; 119 Paul Burns/Photodisc/Getty Images; 120 (t)C Squared Studios/Photodisc/Getty Images, (b)Rubberball/Nicole Hill/Getty Images; 121 Jupiterimages/Comstock Images/Getty Images; 122 Purestock/PunchStock; 123 IT Stock Free/Alamy; 124 Fuse/Getty Images; 125 Susanna Price/Dorling Kindersley/Getty Images; 126 Stockbyte/Getty Images; 127 Sue Scott/Oxford Scientific/Getty Images

MHEonline.com

 SRA

Send all inquiries to:
McGraw-Hill Education
4400 Easton Commons
Columbus, OH 43219

ISBN: 978-0-02-114634-5
MHID: 0-02-114634-9

Printed in the United States of America.

11 12 13 14 15 16 QVS 23 22 21 20 19

The McGraw·Hill Companies

Table of Contents

Table of Contents

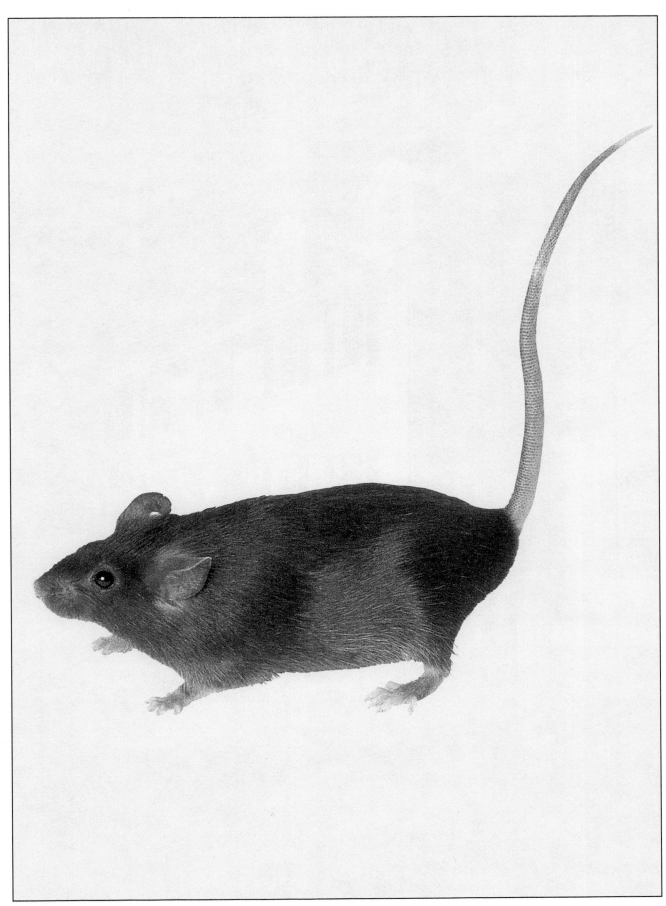

Pictures for Language and Literacy Support, Level 1

Pictures for Language and Literacy Support, Level 1

Pictures for Language and Literacy Support, Level 1

Pictures for Language and Literacy Support, Level 1

Pictures for Language and Literacy Support, Level 1

Pictures for Language and Literacy Support, Level 1

Pictures for Language and Literacy Support, Level 1

Pictures for Language and Literacy Support, Level 1

Pictures for Language and Literacy Support, Level 1

Pictures for Language and Literacy Support, Level 1

Pictures for Language and Literacy Support, Level 1

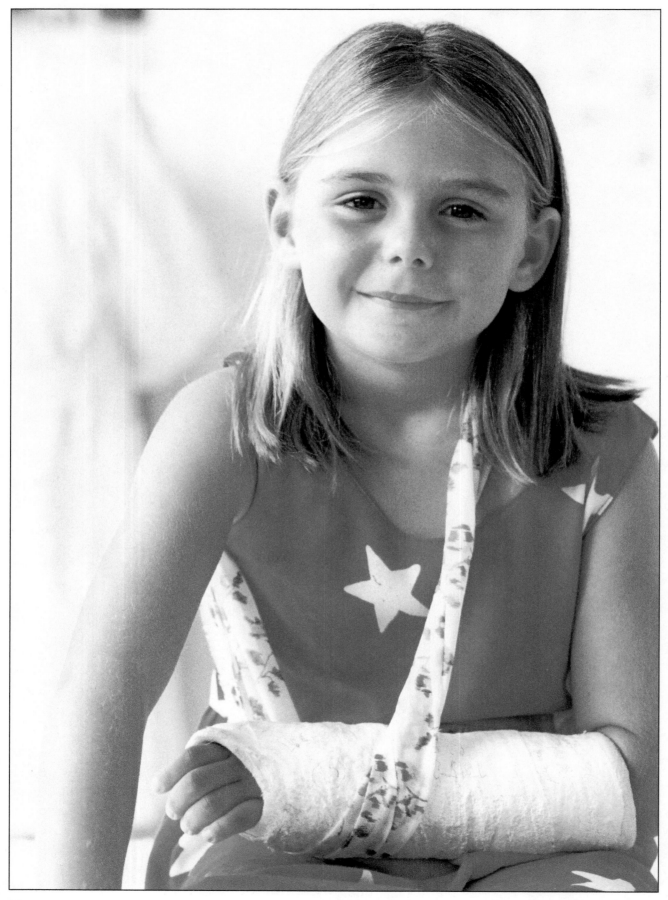

Pictures for Language and Literacy Support, Level 1

Pictures for Language and Literacy Support, Level 1

Pictures for Language and Literacy Support, Level 1

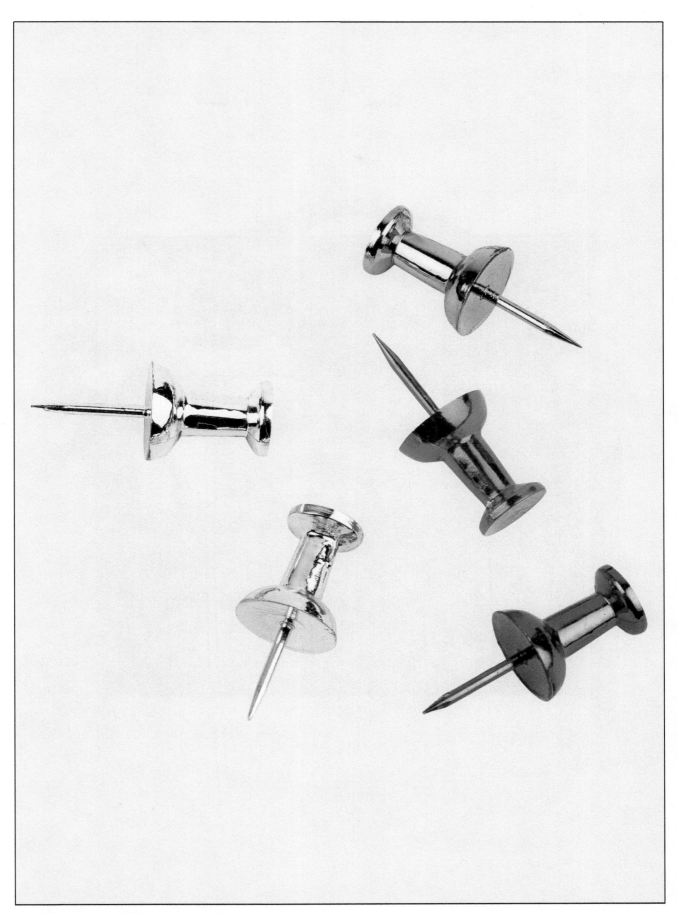

Pictures for Language and Literacy Support, Level 1

Pictures for Language and Literacy Support, Level 1

Pictures for Language and Literacy Support, Level 1

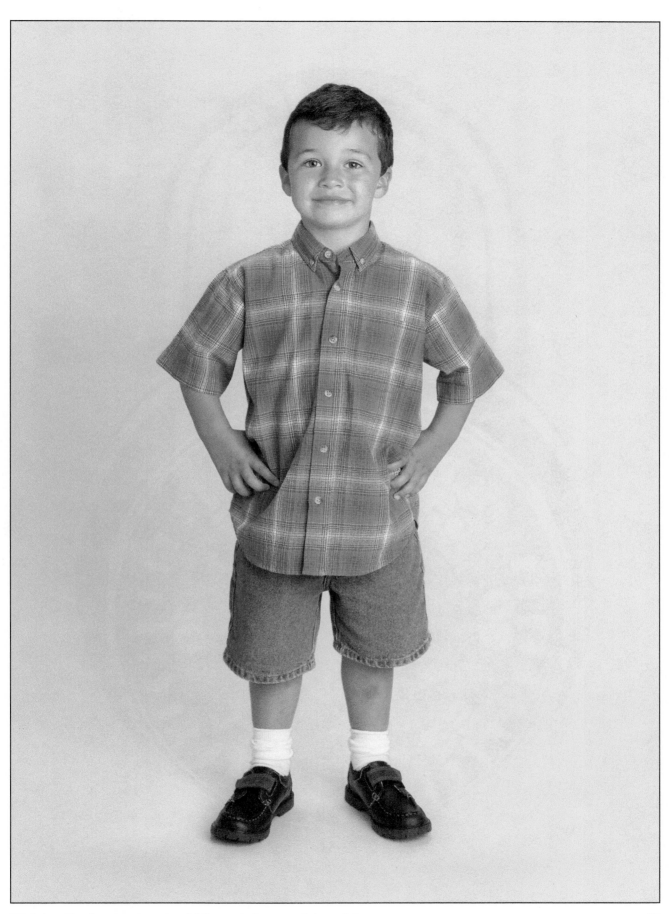

Pictures for Language and Literacy Support, Level 1

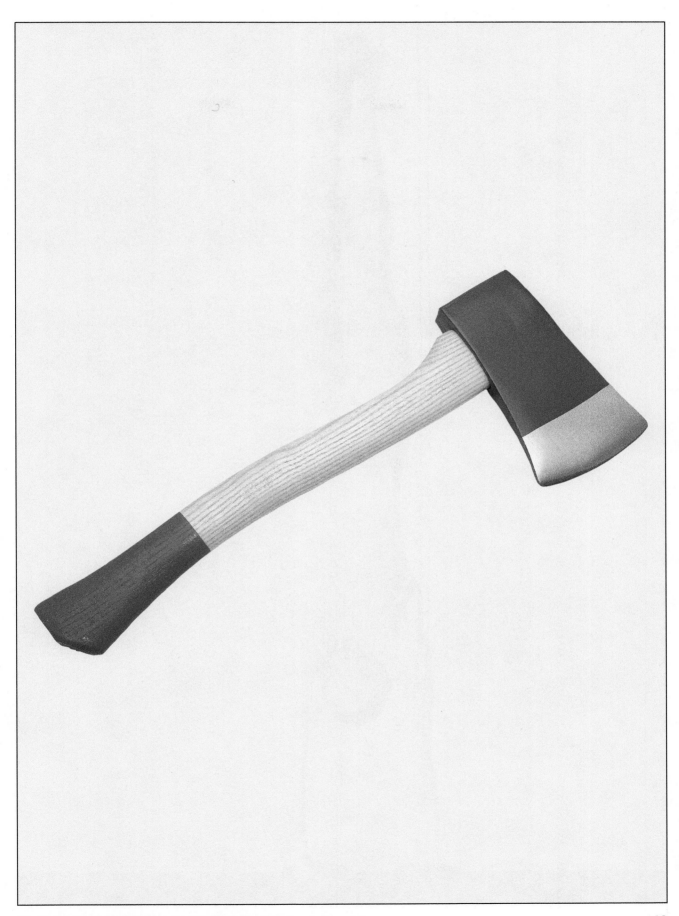

Pictures for Language and Literacy Support, Level 1

Pictures for Language and Literacy Support, Level 1

Pictures for Language and Literacy Support, Level 1

Pictures for Language and Literacy Support, Level 1

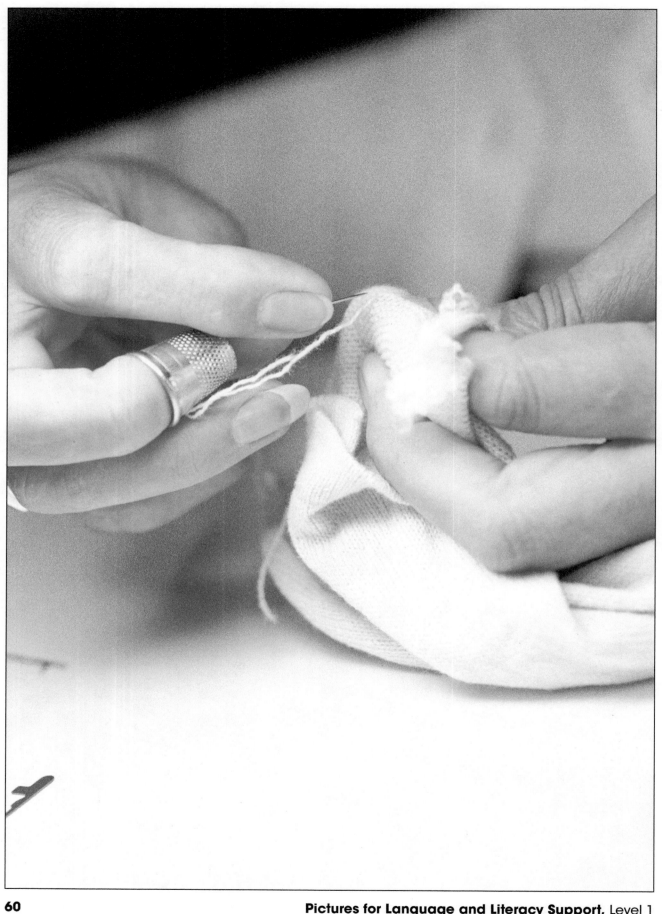

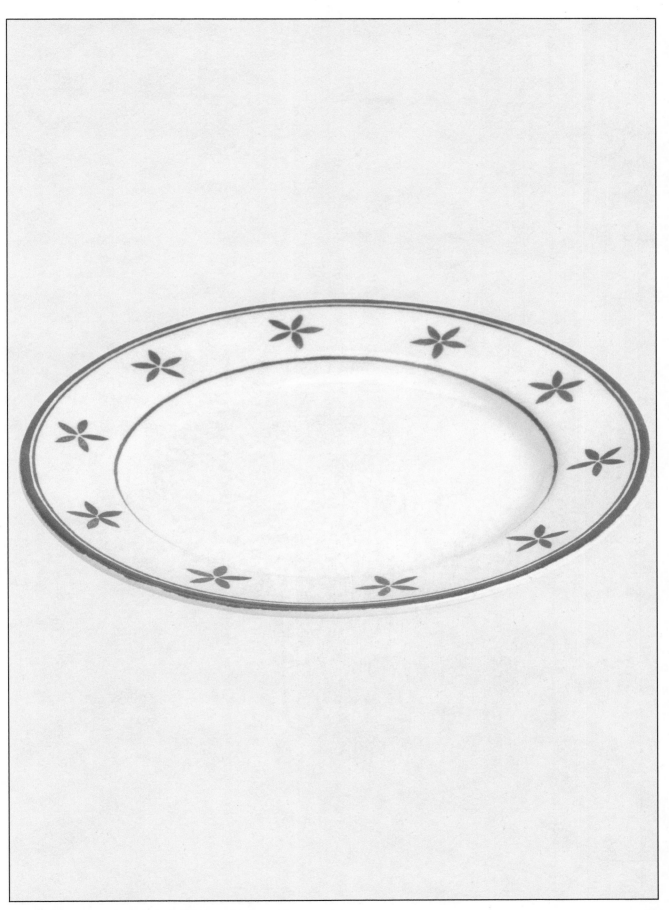

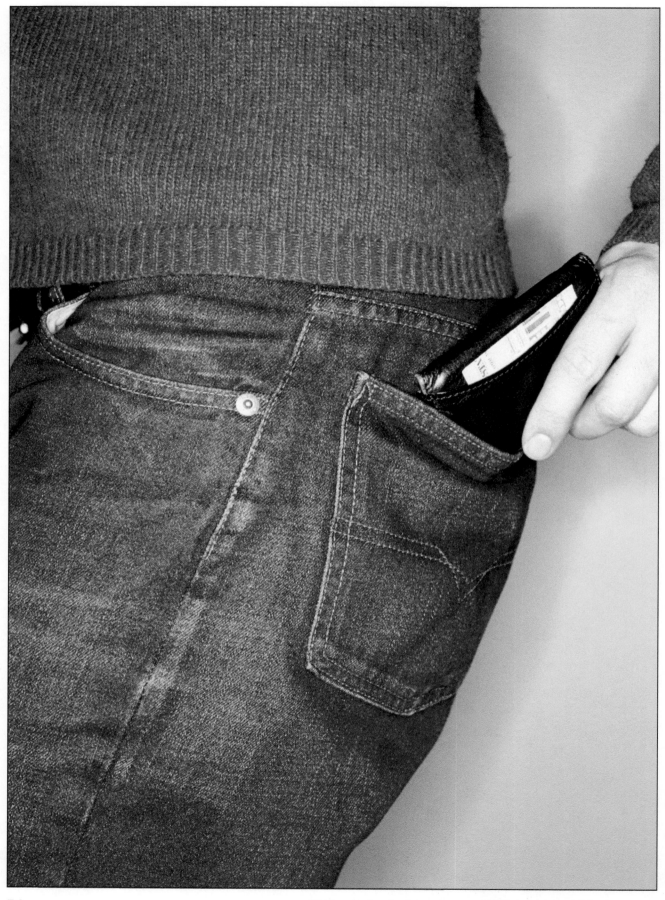

Pictures for Language and Literacy Support, Level 1

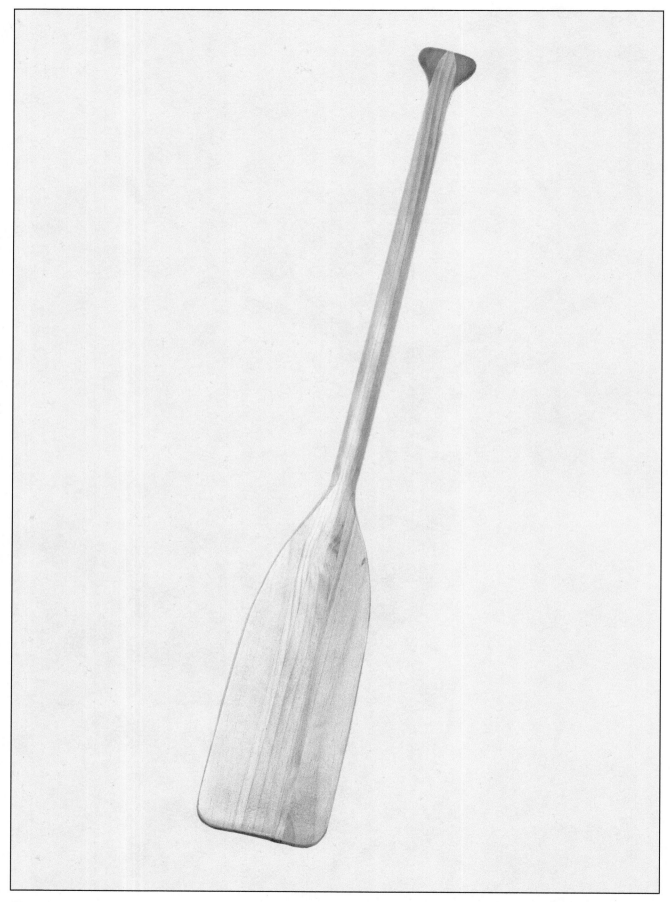

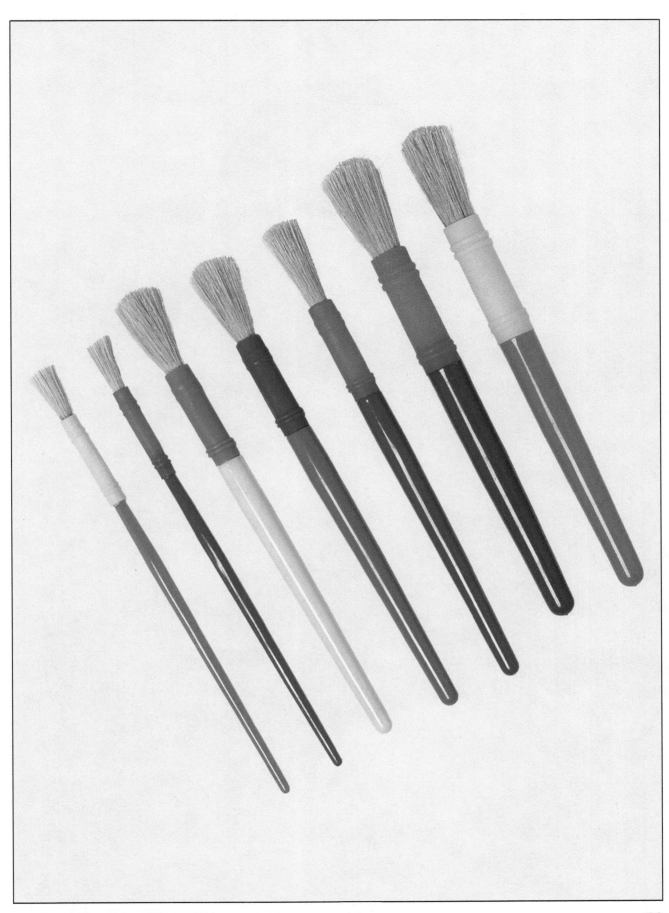

Pictures for Language and Literacy Support, Level 1

Pictures for Language and Literacy Support, Level 1

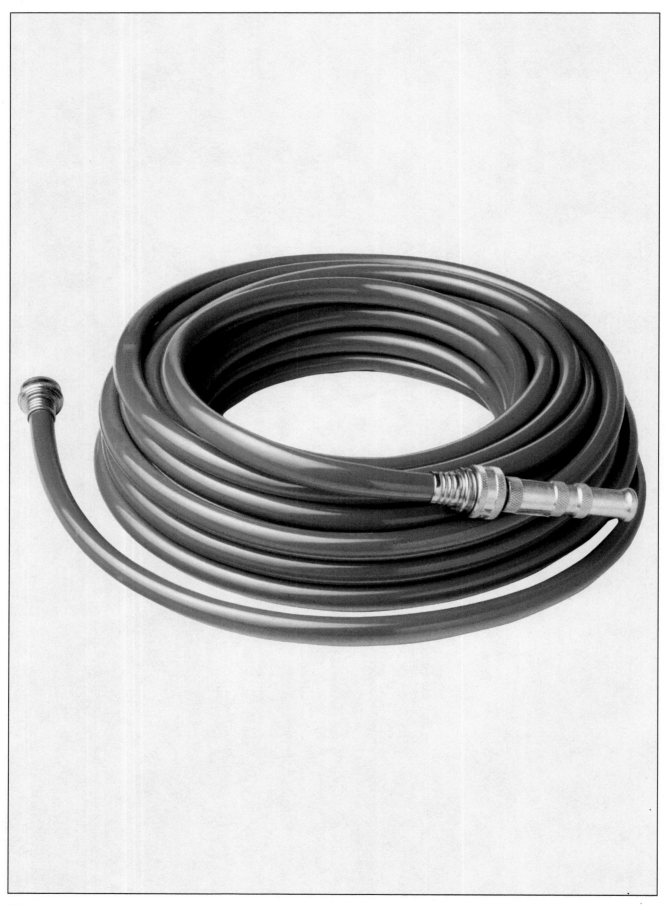

Pictures for Language and Literacy Support, Level 1

92

Pictures for Language and Literacy Support, Level 1

Pictures for Language and Literacy Support, Level 1

Pictures for Language and Literacy Support, Level 1

Pictures for Language and Literacy Support, Level 1

Pictures for Language and Literacy Support, Level 1

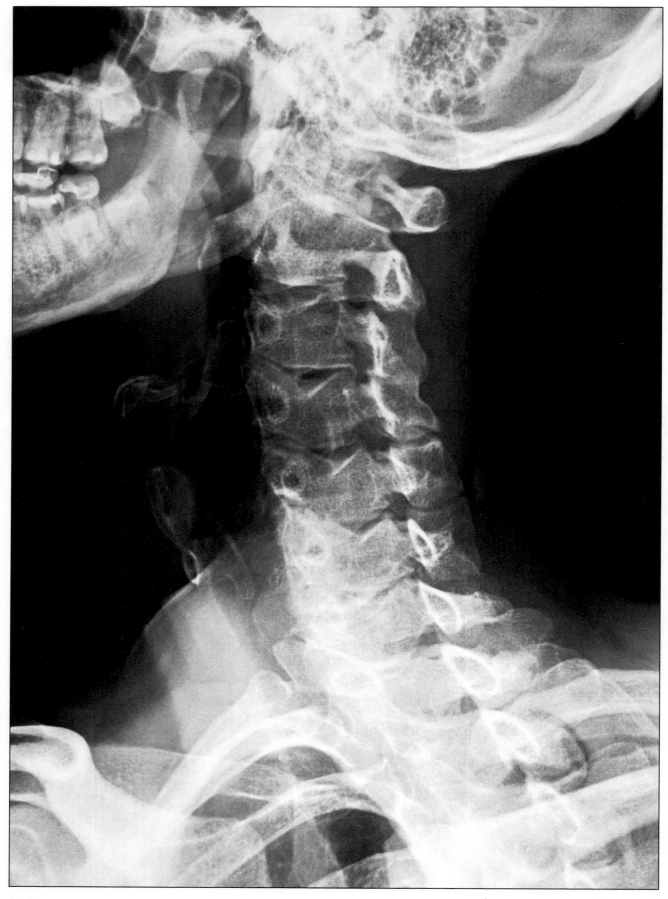

Pictures for Language and Literacy Support, Level 1

Pictures for Language and Literacy Support, Level 1

Pictures for Language and Literacy Support, Level 1

Pictures for Language and Literacy Support, Level 1

Pictures for Language and Literacy Support, Level 1

Pictures for Language and Literacy Support, Level 1

Pictures for Language and Literacy Support, Level 1

Pictures for Language and Literacy Support, Level 1

117

Pictures for Language and Literacy Support, Level 1

Pictures for Language and Literacy Support, Level 1

Pictures for Language and Literacy Support, Level 1